Alive and Taking Names

ALIVE
AND
TAKING
NAMES

AND OTHER POEMS
by Colette Inez

OHIO UNIVERSITY PRESS : ATHENS

Copyright 1977 by Colette Inez

All rights reserved
Library of Congress Catalog Number: 77-86351
ISBN 8214-0377-X (cloth)
    8214-0393-1 (paper)

Printed in the United States of America

MORE FOR SAUL

I would like to thank The National Endowment for the Arts and Humanities, and the Creative Artists Program Services, Inc., for grants which helped me write many of these poems.

ACKNOWLEDGMENTS

The author and the publisher gratefully acknowledge permission to reprint the following poems which originally appeared in these magazines: "Buffalo Sam," *Antaeus*; "Priming the Tunes," *Black Warrior*; "Deanna Durbin, Come Home," *Chowder Review*; "Love in a Silo of Dreams," *Concerning Poetry*; "Nothing is Where the Whiteworm Went," "Twenty Song," *Confrontation*; "Seven Stages of Skeletal Decay," *Cottonwood Review*; "Wavescape," *Epos*; "Mya Calendar with a Debt . . . ," *Hollins Critic*; "Critical Condition," *Ironwood*; "Medico," *Jeopardy*; "He Cooks for Himself," *Kamadhenu*; "The Sky is an English Priest . . . ," *Kansas Quarterly*; "Intercom, Blond in the Wild . . . ," *Kayak*; "I Snapped the End . . . ," "Lieder for a Chocolate Cake," *The Little Magazine*; "Chateauneuf Du Pape . . . ," *Marilyn*; "Aqualove," *Monument*; "The Clam Worm Nereis," *Ms.*; "Old Woman and the War," *The Nation*; "This Stance, This Dance, Distance," *The Niagara Magazine*; "Crucial Stew," *New Letters*; "Alive and Taking Names," *The New Republic*; "Lipprints 1952," *New River Review*; "Home Movie of Poland," "Mundugamor," *New York Quarterly*; "Phenomena, the Oarsman Slides," *New York Times*; "Jungle Queen of Mato Grosso," "Questions for Discussion," "Schoenberg Mosaic," *North American Review*; "Apothegms and Counsels," *Open Places*; "Blind Mouths,"

"Empty Parenthesis," "Far in the Blindness of Time," "November Lord," "Service for Two, I Shall Dine . . . ," *Poetry*; "How I Was Advised by an Elderly . . . ," "Kissing the Lips of Orphanage Girls," "Listening to Dvorak's Serenade . . . ," "Marthe, the Mar, la Mer . . . ," "Overview Choice," *Poetry Northwest*; "Selling Harvesters," *Poetry Now*; "Father Went Out Like a Faulty Fuse," *Quartet*; "When Crinkled, Gold Tin Foil . . . ," *St. Andrews Review*; "Spanish Heaven," "The Zoroastrians," *Salt Creek Reader*; "Rag Dance," *Seneca Review*; "Tektites," *Shaman*; "Skullcraze," *The Smith*; "Old Woman, Eskimo," *Specialia*; "A Skunk in Delaware," *Stinktree*; "Pa and Ma's Rosetime Life," *Sun*; "Diamond Jim and Golden Lil," "Nicolette," *Three Rivers Poetry Journal*; "E Equals M Song," *Vanderbilt Poetry Review*; "The Spring from White to Green," *Yankee Magazine*; "Frocking the Duchess," *Yes, A Magazine of Poetry*: "Tunnel, Funnel, Perpendicular Blue," *Hudson Review*," Priestflight," *West Branch*.

CONTENTS

I

Alive and Taking Names

II

Lipprints

III

Touched in Circles

IV

Doggèd Sources

I

Alive and Taking Names

Thinking of My Father,
Priest, Nightflight to Home

I'm stuffed inside the blandest bird, tuned
to trombones, red clarinets. Who just struck
that plumsweet note? The fruit's thin skin
singing anything but hymnals.

Cities drift, a snaredrum's blur, windy intakes,
the purple horn's recessional under the stare
of those incurable insomniacs, God and the moon.

I've agreed to perform for the Pope
in an aerial Vatican act. Nonsensical Nuncios.
I'm the dunce hungry to love a priest
on an ethereal trapeze, Daddy's stunning acrobat.

But Papa's in an opera box
sweating out the tunes; Gloria Patria,
the scuttling chords of October leaves,
his cassock's sigh in the sacristy.

So many locked away keys, how I fell
from his highwire act into the net of these words,
clues to his ways when he twirled off his collar
and I was conceived, frilled stars, Paris,

neon struts, le hot jazz blowing its stunts
in the fretworks of loss
where my father made the sign.

Kissing the Lips
of Orphanage Girls

What comes to your door?
Walloon girls,
the cold bijou of shattered light
when I was a child
invited to die.

What comes to your door?
The fisherman's son
with a Mako shark
when I was a child
eating davenport legs,
wool in my throat,
stains on my dress.

What comes to your door?
The orphanage man
with a tray of prunes
cockled and black,
the proctor nuns
who scowled at my teeth
biting wafers and blood.

What comes to your door?
The remedy man
who cured my heart
with honey and sticks,
prunes and thick milk
in the bowl of my blood
red as a cardinal when I was a child
kissing the lips of orphanage girls,
Mary Mother and Christ at our door.

Pa and Ma's Rosetime Life

TUPAMAROS, urban guerrillas.
I dream the PA and MA in TUPAMAROS.
Tu is the personal you I call across
subjunctive time. The clock
is running down the page.

Between TU and ROS, those are my folks.
TUer in French is a regular verb.
It means to kill. PA and MA.
Nothing to pry them apart.
Not my wet eraser nor my derringer.

I slump back into light,
the dream balloon swelled up around me.
I, inside its rubber sphere
watching the letters inflate
dark profiles in the air.

They are my fertile parents.
When the cadre sent a ransom note,
they wouldn't pay a sou.
What's a bastard worth?

I sleep like an urban guerrilla
lightly every year,
sending urgent messages
to the leader of my dreams.
TU ES MON PÈRE. TU ES MA MA.
MAMA. A. A. A. Donnes-moi ta ROS(e).

Service for Two,
I Shall Dine with Myself

A crystal teardrop
from the collection
of Madame des Larmes.
I want Dresden.
My voice's alarm
at the front of its box.
The finest Sèvres.
Gold-rimmed everything.

That I was queen of the orphans
when we lived in a burlap sack
everyone knows.
I won't let them forget
the welts I caught
in those corridors.

Service for two,
I shall dine with myself.
Duchess of pity
demitasse cups;
mother-of-pearl on the knives
that I may cut
my mother in half
like a Florida prawn.

This and that Limoges.
I like the word tureen.
What owls say to rats
in Ireland.
It's not enough.
It's not enough.
The fruitwood doesn't match
my dream.

I shall dine with my past,
that chattering child,
plain as a pan
spattering news of peregrine birds.

Take her away.
Put her in a muffin tin
into the pantry and out of my time.
Her parents didn't keep her.
Monsignor La La and Lady Correct
went off to sup on miracles.

Truth Lady, what do you see
in my palm?
Strength of character
and a curious fate
of sidestepping wreckage
in a perishing state.
Nothing gold-rimmed.

The Clam Worm Nereis

deserves our attention
insofar as worms
spur us on to plow for bait.

I've heard women's
private parts called "bearded clams."
Women learn to live in shells
or spend their hours tunneling.
Resemblances end.

Worms. Some mate with their latter end.
Solitary satisfactions of the earth.
Who will love a worm? Fish, hence bait,
birds, hence the early worm catches its death.

Others glisten after rain. Kill them,
kill them. Heavy bodies call for blood.
I guess worms have their way
of uttering muffled, soft, dull screams.

This is fanciful. The ways of the field
swallow our analogies. Not a comment from the stars.
The ways of a worm are odd
if you're not a slug, a snail, a blind, slow thing
poking its path stuttering inch by inch, day by day.

Resemblances begin. Myself segmented into worms,
the long intestines of my words.

Marthe, the Mar, la Mer,
La Mère, Tram, he, rath,
mere, hear my mère,
my mart . . .

We never gave each other groceries.
No brown bags with celery tops,
scouts feeling the air with their leaves.
No leaves between us. You left me with the Sisters.
My father was a brother. My father was a father
to the church.

There were many leaves when we were two.
I, in the branch stems of your veins,
I, red flower, the only one
blooming in the courtyard of your womb.
I howled like a freshly cut rose.
They put me in a vase. I grew fragrant in a country
where no one had a nose.

I, too, am not a mother although once
in a house full of roses, father sky, mother breath,
I left my child with the sisters of death.

Crucial Stew

Crucial, that's me mother's word;
"this is a crucial election."

Christ's been banged
on the crucial with niles,
it were a bloody saight.

"Giscard d'Estaing represents
our highest aspiration,"
me mother writes,

she what
dumped me in an orphanage
in Beljum

is very neat about er person
and as been corresponding
with an English nicetype
for 23 years;
they ain't ever met.

Crucial, Comrade Crucial.
Communist atheist and Kulak killer,
she'd ave said of im.

We're two tough ducks, me and me mum,
she what dumped me with the Catolick Sisters.

Still, crucial, the word, seems a bit
thick and damn the bloody Pope
if I care what wins.

I lost me mother from the start
when they had me stabbing mutton fat
in that groveling pit
of highest aspirations.
Not an eyetheist in saight
but plenty of crucials with niles.

We was very neat about our persons.

I Snapped the End of
My Screaming Hunger

Stalks of smoke
curl my thoughts
to gleaming mother
and a scoured stove
where I snapped
the end
of my screaming hunger
and ran away
to live in a sieve.

Lightly shaken every day
and drained in chutes
of cold grey water,
I peer through the holes
of my hard container
and cry for food.

How I Was Advised by an Elderly Woman to Restrain My Sensual Heat

1. Engrave a NO in sharp, blue ink on the palm of your hand. This is for daytime longings. The NO will drift into your veins, gathering fat. Finally, in its swollen state, a great, blubbering negative, it will squat on your brain where it pumps NO, blue NO. You will sit alone with your paralyzed palm.

2. Dip your wrists under a tap of icy water. Until the skin turns purple and hurts. This is for nighttime longings. Your wrists will freeze into a heavy chain, hearing the hiccups of the clock. Sometimes, you will be entirely restrained, sitting alone, your electric chair wired for its job, but the main fuse blown somewhere out of town.

Nicolette

Nicolette, my little carrot,
I pull you out of the dark ground
of Pennsylvania
where they blasted my thighs
and scraped your seed away.

You are twelve, my counterpart child
breathlessly running into rooms
with acorns and leaves
you want to arrange
for the most senseless beauty.

I have married your father.
We are reconciled to minus signs.

The moist kiss you give me
comes from the forest
of a dark time;

anthracite in the earth,
old signals from the stars
when I walked away from the kill,
blood on my legs, a phrase to caulk
the falling walls in a universe
moving light years away
from our promises.

Nicolette, we will meet
in my poem and when the light
calls your name
you will rise like a fern
to live all summer long,
a green integer
in a pure equation of song.

Empty Parenthesis

I looked for the perfect sentence
balanced as a chain
of plankton, herring, seal. The sentence drifts;
Pribiloff Islands gathering brine
for a comedy of proper nouns.

Labia Majora, constellation in the southern sky.
Binary stars, Clitoris, galactic name.

Better to mind undulant clouds
sweating light as they turn
than to poke the dark with riddles:

yet how does the smile of a crone
put one in mind of the womb?
They both collapse in a future tense
that keeps getting filled
like an infinite parenthesis.

Critical Condition

I hate the stars, spasms of light,
the falling sickness we take as fact
like gravity and dust.

I wanted magnitude,
not the ambulance's scream dying   dying
up the green road.

The summer to swell like a butternut squash,
a green hide to cover the pulp of my fear

but the calendar was stuck,
vines of blood hooked to his skin.
Intensive care I could not give.

My light a corridor of cells
learning pulse by pulse
degradations of the flesh
to fall like a barometer, signalling tears.

My message to the grass, prepare for snow.
The cold is softer than iron beds, than any hospital
weeding its garden of intricate ills.

Medico

Blue medico, you soothe,
white uniform and mask below
the green-spiked irises,
pockets of a foamy brain
where flounders float
and blood is neat,
contained like clams
in bivalve homes,
their room and floor at one.

Late bulletins of light, the stars
flow out into events;
I figure in them like a tick
ingesting cellulose
beneath a cankered bark.

Blue medico, your scoured mind
needs maggots,
bituminous nights to foul your smile.
Go beg, unkempt, but mend my wound,
be god-the-mother to the unkind likes of us,
old clients from the womb.

Alive and Taking Names

If I set out to list ointments
would I find myself slick,
ceaselessly involved
in salves, balms, daubs, smears,
referencing spikenard, lotion, pomade,
greasing the wheels, as it were, of my skin?

Best to forego fat, the oleoginous stuff
that lards the heart.

If I set out to list ills, ague, pox, bloody flux,
would I find myself sick,
ceaselessly involved in croup, rot,
referencing bran, drugging the fool
in the ward of my skull?

Best to forego pain, the surgical brain
doesn't love nouns.

Croaker, monger, medic, quack,
sawbones, prober, jawsmith, vet,
I am well, sound, hale, cross referenced with fit,
snuffling the morning air, alive and taking names.

II

Lipprints

Lipprints 1952

On a poem
keeping their twenty year kiss red,
what shade of the era, Tangee, Dragonfire,
I forget, lipprints from a vanished face
which sailed away and glibly kissed
a random set of signatures, in the script
lilting boys like chords from a tune
in the dancehalls of Paris.
My mouth, the one that pursed over a poem
called "The Unloved."

If I asked those lips to tell the time
they would lie and revise their dim red smile,
coming towards me from a pale of masks,
phantoms in a cool façade of Paris, an album
in blurred frames, vague baroque, the balustrades
corroding even then when I kissed — in the script
mine was the last of the bigtime kissing mouths —
when I kissed late into the night a poem
called "The Unloved."

Buffalo Sam

I loved you a long time,
Buffalo Sam,
your oxblood chukkas
and rifle-hard legs.

Cowhide fingers
strumming the fence . . .
what corrals my eyes made,
circles of stinging dust,
my mouth, a slackened lariat.

Buffalo Sam, sundown clouds
in your cool "adiosito,"
gunpowder light trailing you
to Saskatoon and bunkers north.

Miles were bound to listen
as my body turned to move,
your shadow on its stone plateau,
excavations where I mined
your minerals.

Buffalo Sam,
I loved you a long time,
your malachite heart
and pounding spurs,
bronco dreams I never tamed
in the unsaddled sun.

Love in a Silo of Dreams

Dark as midnight in Sofia, Bulgaria,
my brain embroiders its dreams:

Todor bales the hay. I look for needles
in a stack of days. Time stitches my face.

The hour is soft, my body glides,
a dark bird in touch with a succulent worm.

Blond paths, blond shafts.
Todor is my handyman. I treasure his hands
clenched against the barrel staves,
blinding hills of grass.

Midnight as dark as a saddle
pressed to the flanks of a Romany horse.
Lonesome trails, he sings such songs
from America.

All the farm girls want a chunk of his dreams,
a chance for his love, peppery as sausages.

Todor keeps his counsel, pitching hills
of grain. They say his eyes burn into your skin
like the low blue flame of a candlewick.

He lives in my silo of dreams, a pure gold blend
in the Sofia of my mind.

O Slavic midnight of the heart, enter balalaikas,
enter dervishers in a Sufi twirl, dispersions of light,
his name in the east as I am stunned into love.

Overview, Choice

I put my heart
to looking for your voice
on film,
granular reels, cluster of vowels,
the filmclips in a canister.
Your voice said ahem.

I had cast you as a Sultan,
the soundtrack hummed our names,
sirocco, Algiers, zodiacs turned.
I was your singing Nubian
blue-skinned as a seal.

Overview, wide. I hear the whir.
There's the scene where you sing
Mustafa and his Astrolabe.
Here's the scene where I ride
to the fringe of your oasis

and you sweep me inside
the tent of your realm,
my body like a dune
collapsing under hooves.

Steeds. A shot of sky. The camera pans
the caravan.
Blots on a screen moving in frames.
What was your wish, the Caliph asks.
A dream of water, my low voice blurs
trailing pale cracks in the sand.

November Lord

I have gathered the melons,
my skull is a gourd,
earth, my pumpkin
rolls each night
a hallow's eve
of mindless craft.

A raucous autumn
rattling its stick
on the drum of my skull.
Tight-skinned hours
passive to the sadist baton of the sun.

Ego and grandeur conduct their tones.
I am pitched to love like a crow
ravening the gold harvest.
My sleek coat glistens, bituminous coal
in a mineshaft of shadows.

Where will the find go? Gold in a sieve,
fugitive rock all turning dark,
rituals in a field untended
by the Inca prince, the stunning Atahualpa
in his harvest of death.

Time will comb the gold debris.
Our mouths in the amber of an eon's kiss.
But philologer, my prince sends word,
I cross the bridge into kingdoms of light.
Viracocha, November lord,
the melons are gathered beneath a gaunt moon
which spins like my heart.

Listening To Dvorak's Serenade in E

Everything has ripened,
the oranges glisten
in their sharp worlds,
the apples have broken
their juice
in my mouth,
I am alone at the edge
of all the gold seasons,
a tide of clouds
bearing me home
like a migratory bird.

And this bright music
shaping dancers
on a bitter dust of roads,
divining rods
that point
to a further distance:
stone, water, stone.

Dowser, find my deep stream.
Builder, make my house
to last
in the ochre heart
of the falling sun,
in this shining harvest.

Questions for Discussion

1.
To what extent did you love?
To a large extent in a line
of plovers going south.

How do you justify kisses
coming like plovers from Baffin Bay,
back and forth
between narration and tears?

The omissions that seem most important
aren't here to judge.
Love hovered in the courtroom,
a hummingbird drawn to a perfumed vial.

2.
In what sense of the word did you sing?
Shboom. The setting was significant.
Twenty years of birds
flying south to Uruguay.

How do you isolate the gold dust factor
from problems of flight in a given range?
His flight, my range, home on the sofa
with an antelope's ounce of intention to stay
as opposed to buffalos, as opposed to clouds.

On what grounds did you sight the terns?
In the pearl-grey mantle of the fog.
In our ornithology, he was my finch,
I, his crow. He was my cardinal, I, his nun
flying towards a perfect vow. Christ, I do.

We will meet from time to time
in a garden of Dominicans.
Adios, Brother Gold.
Our vanishing act won't wash
the glittering questions away.

When Crinkled, Gold Tin Foil
Was Wrapped Around
Our Days

Shirley Temple days, her lollipops
and dimpled white strap shoes
tapping the sides of the pool,
we swam and dove in frames

boxed inside a camera
that clicked us unexposed
when we married in summer,

our brown skins laughing
at the parson's drone;
vows a pall
on our flying gainers
and backstroke love.

Almost touched in coats and mufflers,
thin white faces turned away
to see the pool divorced from water,
an open coffin holding snow,

remembering like a film
scissor-kicks and tucks
in the scene where the sun
performs its forward somersault
and we swim into light.

Aqualove

Fishtank of the summer;
we swim in moldy grass,
custard-colored sand,
hours in dark bars
like bruises on the outside light,
slosh our whiskey eyes
thru miles of plastic diatoms,
filaments probing
the reasons we failed
in withered depths
of afternoons,
our childhoods' parasitic ooze
struggling to submerge.
I leap towards the light
but you stay
scratching messages
on the sides of the glass,
your palpable mouth
a feeble grayness in the tank.

This Stance, This Dance, Distance

Even when we were far
there was distance,
lobelias in the field
and changing forms:
elvers into eels,
pupae into moths.

Once we saw blue crabs
clicking under piers,
old boney lovers
along the seawall.
Carapace of sky,
thorax of the world,
they had it in their claws,

the tide flashed in,
what rose fell down,
close things appeared
to be closer than they were:
the rooster's weather vane
rusting on the shore
of those years.

And even when we were close
there was distance,
Crab nebula,
thin claws of light.

The docks disappear
darkened with crowds,
a hammering sound
of bridges forming in the void,
the old blood of clouds
repeating our drift in the world.

Blind Mouths

I look at a circle
of mouths.
Nothing to say.

My grandparents sit
in another blind time,
each in a circle
of worrying eyes.

The children, away,
rolling like hoops,
a distant park
eating their screams.

In the speed of hunger
my parents meet,
two round mouths
to devour their child.

Round as moons
the mirrored plates
reflecting the rooms
in a widening haze
of losses and blame.

The bicycle locked
in the fog of old toys,
wheels, two mouths
of spokes and dust.

Nobody speaks.
The table is cleared.
I look at a field of snow,

the whiteness longer
than I dream,
a blizzard of scraps
confusing the house

large as a van
devouring roads
as it moves through years
pregnant with my furniture.

Twenty Song

When I was twenty
I didn't know the name
of my ways, the sky
walled me in.

I couldn't run out of my body
though I tried racing up dirt roads
to erase my name;
it was blurring downhill
like a sled
carrying the junkpile of my ills.

You were a stick figure
at the top of the hill
offering me shelter
in a stick figure house.

I only guessed the winter
I was heading for, lost
chapters of snow, pale days
like flakes in a rotating storm.
I wanted to throttle the calendar
but the pages turned.   I lived like you
in a pale of change.

Twenty years later
you riffle your light from another time.
I race to catch the fiction of your hair,
what history the stars reported everynight
before I came to where I live,
one in a pair of unmarked dice
in a long, slow roll that seems to win.

Twenty years later
we dance. The red velour room
turns like roulette. I am winning
jackpots, one-armed bandits,
Baccarrat, all my lost games.

What do I want to say?
That I would leave everything
I have made work, rung by rung from the dark
to twirl in the sky of a perfect mirage
where love shuffles its old name in our ear
and we spin.

That isn't it. My message comes from the dark side
of my watch when I couldn't read your hands,
the writing on our walls.
I am innocent as charged and shall comb the bones
of light with your gold hair.
It is late.

Intercom, Blond in the Wild
Gold Success of the World

Assembling resistors, father, daughter, blond, blond,
measures of impedance, red, silver, 1,000 ohms,
two of those, black, silver, 10 ohms, three left,
two of them, father, daughter, assembling resistors,
assembling an intercom.

Capacitors, check them off. This is how the world
will end not in resistance but farads, not in ohmage
but in micro violets, measures of impedance, father,
daughter, two of them, love, love, this is how
the world will end,
metrically correct, checking off the parts,
assembling names, assembling facts.

Who's on the intercom? Who's got the manual?
Time turns us around. Nameplates in the violets,
silver in the voltages and a red silver sun, one left,
check it on the intercom, O my blond loves,
in the wild gold success of the world.

III

Touched in Circles

Old Woman and the War

The conch shell's wall, wheel's hub, moon's rim,
any spoke of asterisk
seems to disappear
like her face switched into darkness
routinely loved by what it touched in circles.

What it touched in circles:
the conch shell's wall and secret fish,
flounders on the moon,
any stalk of sorghum blown
like blind, old lace minutely sewn
over the days of its growing.

Over the days of her growing,
a conch shell's horn summoning believers,
shrines and gatherings of light.
Any look can ransack the events,
a plundered garden and a buried face,
routinely touched by what it loved in circles.

Moon walls, sun's wheel, the conch shell's voice
mustering new armies, routinely felled
and somewhere loved in circles of the word.

Old Woman, Eskimo

Her singing makes
the rain fall.
Her sewing brings clouds.
When she stops sewing,
the green weather comes.
When she stops singing,
the white weather comes
full of smooth threads
to sew up her song.

She has seen birth,
children waiting
for their names.

When she stops seeing,
the snow needles come
sewing the land
to the hem of the sky.
In her dream she is
a bone needle
that will not thread.
The hides come undone,
all her songs are gone
inside the rain
for her children
to hear later on.

Frocking the Duchess

Petits-points there
and a blind stitched hem,
nothing too voluminous.
Why do the scullions dawdle?
This kitchen has been
in my family for 800 years.

The winter before last:
shortages of wood. Auguries of war.
Icicles stabbed the Abbott of Garronne.
He stumbled through the fields
blessing the crows who finished him off.

Peau de soie for the peplum.
Tepid blue as in the blood of my Duc,
Lautrec le Gamin, sterile as a mule
but otherwise grand.
We have made accommodations
to the fertile world.

No godets for the skirt.
I want the ruches plain.
Alençon lace, a snip at the neck.
My throat, dear sir, is firm
and sings Te Deum well as any qua-qua
at the mass.

What impudence! I always pay
when the time falls due. Noblesse oblige.
Last winter Honoré la Robe came to do my sleeves.
Desist. I'll call my valet, Tartare,
easily whipped into curds of desire.

Florentine gussets, one at each breast?
Your eyes, sir, command a surrender
I am willing to make.
Here are my terms.

Chateauneuf Du Pape, the Pope's Valet Speaks

Your mitre must sit well
as the Duchess of Windsor sits well
on her horse,

correctness counts, the crozier gleams,
your chasubles are freshly pressed.

This day reminds me of Moet et Chandon,
little bubbles in a Vatican air,
the sun to kneel in burgundies.
Non vintage champagne for the Bishop of Lièges,
that Flemish hulk of gutturals.
As you say,

we need our zealots, dear Nuncio.
Stay with your bulls. Do not eschew
miraculous fish, the savor of loaves.

This wine is new-fangled,
an impetuous nun. I must confess
to disheveled dreams.

Infallibility calls for meat, steak tartare,
skewered lambs in a shiskabob
from the Levantine.

I once had a prioress in Tripoli kissing
the tongue of my shoe. This wine absolves me
of my infamy. Ah, love that miserere
for two voices.

The room spins its Vatican roulette.
La la la. What wine is this? A bottle
of golden syllables. Yes, your flock clamors
for directions:

norths of venison, Kyrie Eleison, easts of veal,
souths of pork, wests of tripe, papem in aspic,
harum, scarum, cake angelorum,
omnia vincit Armour baloney.

What's that pounding at our door?

The Bishop of Lièges
asks your holiness to bless
the bilingual gluttons of Belgium.

Jungle Queen of Mato Grosso

I am the ravager of innocent celery,
sun rays of carrots, blood moon of beets.
These are my salad days.

Eating a scallion, Cleopatra
in her loud green breath
submitted to the dynasty of death and escarole,
green salad earth tossed into space.
The salad of jungles.

I am the jungle queen of Mato Grosso,
blue eyes from the blanco
who entered the outpost, science on his side,
and submitted to raids, outsized butterflies
sapping his mind.

Plucking lice from his blond crop,
my mother, a Tupi, caressed his film,
lenses, cassettes, the Mozart LP,
ravagers of silence and flashbulb time.

Those were her salad days, endive, romaine.
Persiflage and twitting wit loudly absent
in the hut where blanco's skull hung on a pole
next to his bufferin, quinine and notes
on the dreamtime of Tupis.

Mundugamor

He comes in a cape of steaming rain,
Mundugamor, my father, chief.
His tattoed body slashed like rain
and arrows in the village.

I sit by a thatch naming the rain
and call to my father
who entered my mother
in a village dream
harvesting taro.

Many rain palms waving the forest.
My tapa skirt is old.
I have young brothers slim as rain,

their knives like a silence
ready to speak.
In the burial rain
our mother's body rubbed with clay,
set in caves of long, gray dreams.

I call to my father.
I, his orchid in the feasting years,
sweet potato, conch,

before my brothers cried into life
and our mother went far
like an empty canoe
to caves of long rain
in the night.

Diamond Jim and Golden Lil

Her spaciousness and Brady's paunch
had never read cholesterol
in the early heart of July
seeing wheels of fire on the river.

Ain't it grand, Jim said,
she'd stripped her corset off
to down a dozen oysters,
three boiled lobsters
and raspberry ice.

To the common watchers
of artistic light,
they were pinpoints of fame
in a distant house.

Diamonds in her throat
furbishing the highest note,
Lil sang to the glitter of things
winking like Brady's pinky rings.

When they left the world's table
champagne sighed
addling diners
who said, ain't it fine

how Lil and Jim
pried time for its pearls,
their ground like a shell
for the pie of the world.

Phenomena, the Oarsman Slides
Under My Eyes

Netted for an instant,
the body seamed, soldered to a sea
which bears him like a follicle
in its green hair;

maybe a broken mind
hoisted in a sling
but mendable,
repairing in the wind.

His boat a means to sputter
an undetected time,
a shutter's fold
which snaps him in
out of the crowded center.

Somewhere his nerve lines pulse
like crumbling neon as he floats,
prisoner of limits and the chance
the tide will drag like packaging
the life he had to bring.

His time released to look elsewhere
inside the sea
which holds no more of a clue
than when he came
examining.

Deanna Durbin, Come Home
(Deanna Durbin was born in Canada
and now resides in France)

We melted; liquid cherry centers,
vanilla-colored lozenges
in balconies,
emporiums of movie dust,
committed the dark to memory

as Deanna beamed, Funiculi, Funicula
in her strapless gown
fluttering High C
to our hicktown's popcorn litter.
It was a better world of bluebirds,
usherette bliss, rectangular light
as the screen snapped on
in the umptyum years.

Deanna Durbin. The columns say
she parles with the crème de la crème
in France. Entre nous, quel ennui!
I wish she'd come home. The Mounties hunt
her trebled notes out near Lake Louise.
Time takes a breakneck tour of whatever happened
to whom and where. Despotic love of memories.

Deanna Durbin. I want her baby orchid throat
singing GOIN' HOME, the way it used to be
when the light poured in like a blizzard
and I floated home humming the theme,
unblinking faith in moviehouse shrines,
transparent ends, wholehearted gods,
    Funiculi, Funicula.

Priming the Tunes

**(for my foster uncle Ed who tuned
pianos for the theatre trade)**

Vandeville marquees,
a neon alphabet of hits and flops,
it was long ago in a garden of tricks,
blue octaves of dusk,
in a season of arpeggios,
July Fourth rippling into arcs.

You are a bluebird, my uncle said,
and we drank summer potions
in long silver nights.

Tunes, tunes. Tap, tap. Bravos and hoots.
The dancers have spun down the stage
to a thin wax of light.
The red velvet curtain in a miracle
of parting.

Tricks, tricks, pale words flake
on a shabby stage.
My uncle's scorched gold hair
gone in a burnt out case of pine.

Runaway hoops, how many moons?
It was long ago,
there were firefly guides
in the theatrical dark of my love.

Bluebirds are rare, he went on to say,
coaxing a tune from the upright.

He Cooks for Himself

After the clatter Yetta made
he wanted no news
to knock down his door

and counted on silence
in the dregs of his chair,
the room's cloth coat
to warm like fur

but the walls kept calling
do this, do that.
Yetta like a spatula
scraping his silence.

How to scrub her face away?
He daily frayed
like trouser cuffs,

nightly saw the kitchen float
in vegetable fumes,
the gray sink gurgling Yetta's dream
of a tidy God, angelic soup,

and resigned himself to facts:
she's in the pipes
shouting for a plumber,

Drano won't revive her
nor onions and cabbage
in a constant quarrel
with the boiling water.

Spanish Heaven

My heaven is Hispanic ladies in satin tube dresses,
their hair like a chocolate sundae melts into waves.
They are giving me transparent nightgowns
and kisses on my face.
Lotteria tickets bulging in my purse.
They are saying *que bonita* in the house
of their throats
and we all eat mangoes and fritos d'amor
selling Avon products to each other forever.

And damning Fidel, Trujillo, what bums.
But Evita, what heart and Elizabeth Taylor
there in her shrine,
Monacos of pleasure as Grace takes our hand.
Eyepads of freedom, Avons of love.

Mascara of angels, hairspray of God,
they are teasing my hair like a heavenly cloud
while the acid of husbands eating alone
rumbles Dolores, *putas* and rape
in the hell of machismo.

The Sky is an English Priest
Undoing His Coat

Holy orders, to hell with starch,
my too stiff life making its rounds
like a laboratory coat
from one sickbed to another.
What the priest said
at summer's end
facing corridors of snow,
the doors marked closed
to healing love.

Better to undress, be a jade
where the sea coruscates its green,
to peel off hours like
an old stripteaser
waiting to burn on a coast of sand.

Rain, rain sound your applause.
What the stripper said
at the platform's edge,
defrocked on the street Sweet Jesus Saves
for a slouch of men.
Bad weathers of autumn surely to come
before the Messiah.

Selling Harvesters

Man: Self-propelled combines
to harvest small grain,
covers 60 acres in a day.
Cutter bar attachments,
forage for silage,
getting in the crop.
Selling harvesters is tough.

Woman: Do you remember the December Society?
Duane and I danced a lot.
I wore my sweater set and pearls.

Man: I want to put it in writing.
I seldom have the chance
to express what's on my mind.
One thing, I've gotten to do
what I set out to say
even when I felt
exactly what I meant
but couldn't say it.

Woman: He was always away.

Man: When I first started in the world
I said "could be, could be"
about people, all their savings
around the table.

Woman: Pomona, Sonoma, Solano.

Man: We all had ice water at dinner.
          Mother made a roast.
          Father told me to eat less
          so we'd have enough.
          There's a lot of jealousy and conflict
          in selling harvesters.

Woman: I loved watching him
          open packets of sugar.
          Very neat. A wrist watch on his wrist
          to check out the time.

Man: I think I'll write
          we were suspenseful strangers
          in an unformed plot,
          both of us from different ruts
          criticized and groomed
          to look things up and trust.

Woman: My watch isn't right.

Father Went Out Like a Faulty Fuse
(for Saul)

For company, only the rain
cleaning the roof, the wall's bad breath
as lamplight drives the darkness out,
corners my rage in a straightback chair.

Nothing to say, the oilcloth moans
under the swack of Mother's sponge.
The dirty hour won't come clean;
I want my father, my father back.

He won't come home and Mother sweeps
noodles and broth into my sleep.
Ladling kisses, her spoon-shaped mouth
feeding my eyes fortified love.

He's burning a hole in the frazzled air
basements away on an island of games,
pinochle roots and poker palms,
stranded from Mother and me in her arms.

I go to dream the odds are good
he's gone to singe a random star
with his fat cigar galaxies away.
I'll catch him through a telescope
after the rains.

Rag Dance

The house has a runny nose,
fever in the yard.
The ragpicker's daughter
has caught a blind cat
and is teaching it to sit.
She doesn't succeed.
The house runs down.
The cat runs off.
Only the sky
stays in its place
teaching the girl
to run like a cat.
Love runs down.
The light learns night.
Only the dark
teaches the blind
to love what they have.
Only the blind
stay in their place
to have what they love
in the dark.

Lieder for a Chocolate Cake
(for Herb Leibowitz)

Weimar Republic, Bauhaus scroll, an afternoon
of sweets and wine before the Gauleiters rise
and Einstein is gone quickly as a formula for time,
before the stench of the Reich widens in a trail

to Kristalnacht. There are Jews
with quivering blonde curls
ramming rubies down their throats
as a Berliner whore gorges on cake
knowing the untermensch who pays
will gasp over her body like an evil storm.

Every crazed taste sated, the swastika rules,
Hitler hugging dogs, Eva taking shots
of edelweiss in bloom, Himmler jigging
in Wehrmacht boots as they enter the castle
to eat swirled cakes rich as cartels.

We have survived the firestorms and are intact,
alive to examine the volatile joy
of this chocolate cake sitting before us
like a reward for being good in the thunder
when our mouths watered for surrender,
parents to fall
on their knees for our love, in the long fever
of being a child pleading for an armistice
the world refused to sign.

Home Movie of Poland

A picnic table. The family assembles.
As if in a dream you are small,
your cousin squints, his shredded hair
later deloused at Bergen-Belsen.
Grandfather swatting flies. It is summer,
gentile, undulating blond.
Grandma sews a button on.

Nearby, the house stoked with bread
warm as the bed
you and mama slept in
like a closed parenthesis
in Poland's sad, long sentence.

Elsewhere, the Fuehrer's bloody moon
rising in Sudetenland, plans for decimation.

They were so old, Noah and Sarah,
old and thin as rain,
easy to close the valve of their lives
as he bent to the news like a birch in the wind.
Grandma seizing her only hen
for a future of eggs. Auschwitz freight.
Jerusalem, if I forget thee,
let me lose my right arm.
God has plucked you out of the disease.
The frames fade, white phlox and blood
shedding their scent in a closet of dreams.

Rescued.
That your mother and father
hunched in a room to make you come true
like a glistening egg,
that you will not crack
for any Wehrmacht omelette.

Your hair fringed like Polish stars
in a telescope of nights
when the moon was removed to Bergen-Belsen
in the final solution of moons.

Do not forget Jerusalem,
my love in a western land,
America, America where we live in a film
spooling forward and back in the speed of events —
unreal as the light
that blinks in our eyes after hours of darkness.

Nothing is Where
the Whiteworm Went

Nothing is where the whiteworm went,
crouched into wormwood and dust.
Existence, taped in inches
through yards of stone is lost.

Once I saw the whiteworm
stuttering softly in turf,
curled on a leaf by the greenhouse
where orchids choked in loam.

A slither at my throat
and in my jail of flesh
I stomped, stomped the omen down,
ground the worm to mash.

But menaces survive
enfeebling my defense.

Seven Stages
of Skeletal Decay

0-5   Centers of ossification appear as I squall
"wyde in this world wonderes to hear."
The light my second amnion.
Mother like a frog, white exhausted thighs
precede my deciduous teeth, the better to bite
the asylum where I didn't earn my keep.
Ward of the state and stable criteria.

5-12   Acetabular elements join.
Ilium, ischium, pubis,
a little hen's breast against my hands.
In the corpulent dark hearing children grow
a song of bones as the moon climbed
and ovary bells, my eggs and the moon
tolling each month.

12-15   Epyphisial union of long bones.
Long bones in my stride,
glib nights, counterfeit smiles,
trumped-up charges against what I loved.
Years blindly eating childhood's fat.
Knowledge like a shield
wounds when pressed too near.

25-36   Active vault suture closing.
Active designs in the skull.
Delicate zippers sealing in
the stars, interstellar dust,
brackets of marriage, and one short birth
shaped like a comma between two worlds.

36-50 Lipping of scapular glenoid fossa.
Fossa, a ditch.
I have not come to it.
Fossa, an abyss.
I wait for the master archeologist
to dig and pick,
tweezers plucking artifacts,
my trail of refuse and souvenirs.

50 plus Quasi Pathological erosions of bone.
The pendulum's pit.
My old electrons blow their fuse.
Dark pond.
My mother like a frog,
white exhausted thighs collapsed.

plus What did it mean to play
a xylophone of bones?
An octave of stone. Delight. Decrease,
bleached lips dim against my fingers
closing in a stiffening fist,
dumb warrior
pitted against eloquent death,
illiterate mulch for those whose squalls
will go "wyde in this world
wonderes to hear,"
the light their second amnion.

IV

Doggèd Sources

Skullcraze

A mulish sky that plowed its heat
on every facet of my space,
perversely tuned and hitched to light,
I saw it pull the grazing sun
downcourse as the afternoon
rolled its crop of darkness.

Minute implosions crazed my skull,
I danced a spastic waltz and loved
scrub, nettles, briars, gorse
intractable as school
where the sun like a melon
hid in its rind.

Miles in furrowed rain
where I danced the time my memory took;
thorns, pods, addertongues,
toadflax, vetches, milkweed, fleas
moving mules through damn
questions of existence,

and rode the mule like Christ to love
all doggèd sources.

Tunnel, Funnel,
Perpendicular, Blue

Morf. The dog barks.
Form for the poem.
Meop, the cat.
Listen to the apertures.
Look for the throat that shapes the bark,
the mouth of the cat.

Anything, therefore, is form
emerging from that which informs.
And uniforms:
an usherette in the theater of signs,
an Argentine pilot plotting the stars.

Stars form. Blue young, red old,
go out dwarfed in the inverse dark
astronomers seek seeking form.
Morf. Morpheus. Sleep has shape:

tunnel, funnel, perpendicular, blue
foldout map that continues to blur
under the glass of a witnessing mind.
Breakneck turns. A cur, occur.
Form determines the speed of turn.
Deeps of return
continue to blur what precision occurs
when the pump erodes and no blood climbs,
condemned to its fact as the brainstem pales
like a blasted stalk, and the brain won't bloom.

Obedience bows to formula's rule,
to its chemical investiture
and what we call silence has the noise of a shell
informing our ears with the sea of itself.

Not wordless dogs. Listen to the harnesses.
Look for the hand that shapes the whip,
the arch, the crucifix
in a mastery of form.

Schoenberg Mosaic

Schoenberg, iceberg,
the odor of music resembles God
in its diffusion, a dog in its confusion.
Confusion say: Currier Ives for Charles.
New things don't soothe.

There's a future in your tomorrow
and old scales to play unless you change
your ear's address.
That iceberg is Goliath
after hearing David's lute. His ear was gross
and lost to points. The skua gull reports
what nuances he needs: plankton, snow,
the humming seals.

In stalags of the north
terns avoid what staves they can.
An odor of dogs resembles loss.
There's a past in the presence of your home
in a contract no one signed, Schoen Time
Konzert Krieg twelve tones ago.

Odors of snow when the agent is God
selling tundras to dogs of his alternate choice.
And the ice in choice adamant as tone, epitome
and other sounds in the Schoenberg rungs
of twelve toned climbs, Eine Kleine Nacht bergs
in God's white blood
soaking the darkness with snows of his love,
and la la's of stars.

Apothegms and Counsels

If someone says you're too short,
say diamond pins don't come in cartons.

If someone says you're too large,
say you're an Amazon at large.

If someone says your breasts are too big,
say you bought them in Katmandu
and the fitting rooms were dark.

Say chickpeas are loved in Prague
if someone says your breasts are too small.

How much do you weigh on the sun?   On the moon?

Tons on the sun.
Less on the moon.
Love makes you weightless.

If someone says you're too far out,
say Doppler Effect,
that you're writing a history of light
for the children of Pythagoras.

E Equals M Song

One cocked pleasant hen
hasn't read the time
her blood will write
in the afternoon.

One crocked peasant
measures his wine,
its known dimension
crumbling pain.

One shocked pheasant
studies his wounds.
The afternoon ends
in a barnyard of stars.

Cockle doodle moon
and dawn again.

Limits in the universe,
coops cackling doom,
pleading sheds of calves
and hogs.

The peasant dreams
Vienna to stop the station at 3.
E equals M, Dorking hens
melt in the speed.

One pocked peasant,
his drunken twin
waiting on the tracks
for the train to begin
what is known.

Mya Calendar with a Debt to Birney's "Janissary, Cassowary, Marsh"

Monks of the Years for Zodiacal Ears

Actuary, Fritillary, Mush
Mandrill, Mace, Jejeune,
Jelly, Aghast, Septic Ember,
Oak Toner, Remember, Distemper

Device to Mesmerize the Monks

30 days hath septic ember
mandrill jejeune and remember
all the rest have 31 dyes
of different color:

Actuary: puce   Mush: buff
Mace: rose   Jelly: lime
Aghast: jade   Oak Toner: rust
Distemper: slush

except Fritillary which howls
28 cold tones of dust.

Tektites

Black crusted shrapnel,
they are not known to wound,
and occur in strewn fields of Luzon.

Astronomers believe
they are particles of moon
in fields of Luzon,
Alabama, Canada, the Nullarbor Plain.

Shaped in passage,
they are particles of moon.
Astronomers are shaped
in their passage to Luzon,

Alabama, Canada, the Nullarbor Plain.
In a passage through shrapnel,
men are known to wound
and occur in strewn fields.

A Skunk in Delaware

The odor is his armor
and speaks plain speech.
Miles will eat the stench
as drivers flash
on striped roads
smelling a memory of the sea
where skunk and men
in a protein heat
fumbled for land, sperm to the womb
of the future tense.

The sea, meanwhile,
spells Delaware stone
slow as the turtle
that holds the world,
the skunk that mocks
the moon's design
of wide light on the water.

The Zoroastrians Knew

The Zoroastrians knew
how men coax shadows,
the story of luck in a garden, frangipani,
what woman was arranged, oleander, musk
for what man at dusk, all for the good of Mazda.

It is written in the dunes, camels dream of clouds,
routine recalcitrance under their hooves.
Magisterial clouds, gathering words
like a memory of travel
in the sand.

The Zoroastrians knew
what depth of moonlight moved
whose secrets into dawn. A freshly loved clue
rooted in the dark where a woman slept
lightly as a guard jangling the keys to her prison.

A luckless garden in her past, frangipani, dew.
Her master like a whip dreaming of fame.
The bride like a hide, her transient name
sold to the merchant of shadows.

Far in the Blindness of Time

The day passes from nearness into distance.
First, the sun, then the stars.
Sounds carry far on the water.

The contained are asleep in their clouds
but the young are like fire,
orange and red tongues in the dark
igniting the old from the fog of their dreams.

The boy points his knife.
First, the stars, then the sun.
Blood makes no sound on the water.

The contained are asleep in their clouds.
A boy is pointing to the water.
He and his friend darker than hawks
skimming the light, out of reach.

Wavescape

My glinting water,
the ramshackle beach
and its raggedy coast.
That diamond tide
is a meadow of fire
the sky puts out
at dark.

I run, an unsteady courser,
wrecked dunes behind me,
events in a drift.

It will not take me in
nor will I spin
my wrongheaded heart
in its mouth.

A shambling blur
where the mainland slopes,
rotting signs.
The seaboard disrobes,
naked stone.   No accord.
Mother of Christ,
praise the sea's gain
in my stay; unending days
in the risk of the waves.

The Spring from White to
Green Equations

No end, said the sky,
snowed in, no wending
allowed from that odd
numbered house.
My last hen cackled
and even she walked
a logarithm I couldn't solve
on the whiteboard of the storm.
I was stuck in an acre of snow.

Now wild algebra
in the hummingbird's dervish.
Predicaments of rain.
A crack in the gate
lets flood my hen, winebottle flies,
a hubbub of bees.

I spring from white to green
dilemmas, no solutions from the vines.
The robin stands his ground
with worms. A puzzlement of butterflies,
my old dazed hen.

Then what's the cure?
No mending, says the sky,
the end, says the sun
grinding the light for my bones.